The Beekeeper's Wife

Shanda Hansma Blue

∞

Published by:

Suite 300 – 852 Fort Street
Victoria, BC, Canada V8W 1H8
www.friesenpress.com

For information on bulk orders contact:
info@friesenpress.com or fax 1-888-376-7026

Distributed to the trade by The Ingram Book Company

I dedicate this book to my husband Robert W. Easterday, and to our children, Danyi Heckaman Beldavs, Morgan Genevieve Blue, Graydon Courtney Blue, Kerry Easterday Olvera and Eric Easterday.

Table of Contents

Acknowledgements

Thank you to my husband Robert W. Easterday for his love and support.

Thank you to Herb Scott and Shirley Clay Scott, both loving, thoughtful teachers and mentors.

Thank you to the publishers for the following poem publications: "Waves and Particles." the *Dos Passos Review*; "Revision", *Dislocate* Fall 2004; "Internal Bleeding", *The Louisville Review* 2000; "Ballet," *The Southern Indiana Review* 1996; "The Maple Wood," *The Southern Indiana Review* 1995; and Thinking About High School", *Southern Indiana Review* 1994.

The Beekeeper's Wife
Herbert Scott

She wakes beside his body brown as bees.
Why can't he know? She wonders as she waits
why loneliness must be a private thing.
If she could send the messages she keeps
her hands would tell him of her aching bones,
her mouth would be the only sound he knows.
Outside, the queen is dead, the shifting trees
are warm with bees and ripple with the wind
of wings. Oh she would be the keeper's girl
and run with lifted skirts to gather them
and hang her heart upon a leaf- blown tree
to house them in and feed them on her blood.
But, could she bear the weight of their blind love?
Some nights she thinks the sound will never stop,
or dreams the bees are netted in her hair.
One day she saw them fill a calf's skull, bring
the bleached bones back to life, become the eyes,
the living tongue that cries. Why can't he see
her body is alive? Why won't he wake
to heal her given wounds? She moves along the bed
and touches him, and waits for him to know
the torture of her fingers, where they go
There is a fluid movement to his sleep.
She feels his body swarm across the sheet.

Scott, Herbert. "The Beekeeper's Wife".
Disguises 1974 University of Pittsburg Press.

White on White

Sunrise was just at that height
where the lake was lit, pale gray
and white, not yet blue,
a sun-imbued cloud settled
on the water, filled our little valley,
invisible lake, white on white,
no horizon. We saw from our window
framed by dazzled oaks, cottonwoods,
two swans at their morning swim
from the cloud bank, slowly
become visible, talking to themselves,
swimming toward our shore
as if in the cloud, in the sky,
white on white, no horizon.

Angle of Reflection

Outside my car, in a sky clear
like a blue-black bowl,
the brightest sliver moon shines through
the passenger corner of my windshield.
Why does our singular moon have a generic name,
like "man" for human,
not reflecting the multiple brands of race
or gender on this planet,
unlike the multiple moons of Jupiter?

As I turn my face to look out
my driver's side window and up,
I see a fuzzy anomaly that I think
is Hyakutake, described by astronomers
surprised to see it while searching
the heavens for Eros. They sight not
the Greek god of love but an asteroid
of unstable orbit, a comet ten miles in diameter,
a dirty space ball that science surmises
would make a crater the size of New York state
if it hit our Earth, would make a cloud
of debris, a shaded world, and stunt
all earthly growth for years.

I turn down a county road toward
my favorite pond, low road, high water,
sliver moon and Hyakutake reflected
among reeds and drowned trees
in the bottom of this bowl,
to see if I can spot the first
frog-fishing heron of spring.
Instead I see mud hens
like dark brown bobbers treading water
nearly up to the center of the road
and beyond them, lapped by the pond,
the glow of a possum
anticipating resurrection.

Waves and Particles

She lives in the five percent zone
of northern lights visibility. She thinks
of this as her numerical data,
her location on the statistical
halo of Earth's auroral latitudes.

When the beekeeper wakes she's at a north-
facing window. She rises from their bed
at one thirty or two a.m., looks out,
hopes for a shimmering of magenta
light bright enough to obliterate stars,
but this is a rare mid-night vision.
When she points them out he mistakes
those glowing regions, auroral patches,
for small clouds in the night sky.

She anticipates the magnetic storm
that expands the one hundred percent zone,
brings the instantaneous oval
toward her latitude, her purview,
so she can look skyward for green arcs,
blue bands, rainbow-colored veils and rays
as they pulse and flame the sacred night.

He anticipates an uninterrupted
night's sleep, tempts her with warm milk
and honey. She daily watches the sun's
weather, solar flares and coronal masses
ejected toward this planet, until
the electrons and protons of solar wind
transforms the world's magnetic field
into a vast weather vane that splashes
light around the auroral oval.

Waves and Particles

She wants to tend the light particles
of the aurora borealis the way her husband
tends his bees. The way honeybees drape
their swarm on the outside of the hive,
cluster in their door-opening, she wants
to watch these lights drape their rose-glowing
corona around her house, fill every window,
each doorway, until her soul rides space-ward
on their waves, until he wakes and his gravity
draws her back into their zone.

Pastoral

As she drives by on the highway she sees,
parked in the semi-truck pullout, rest-stop,
two of those out-sized yellow salt spreaders
that help keep the road clear in winter,
cabs side by side, so the drivers can roll
down their windows and talk to each other.

The trucks are like two huge brightly colored
horses muzzle to muzzle, rubbing faces,
neck caressing neck, the steamy plumes
from their exhaust pipes like gaily waving
tails when Spring is coming.

She Hunts Alone

There is little to do for bees in spring
after harvesting honey from hives
that died in winter, so she hunts,
a single stalker she leaves less
human smell and track in the woods
and fields. Even pea-brained wild turkeys
are elusive, avoid signs of human society,
but this spring she has a new matte black
shot-gun guaranteed not to reflect
a hint of her presence before a bird
is in range. She takes her backpack
ready to lug poultry out of the woods,
sets out each morning with her collection
of mouth, box, slate and tube calls to tempt
a large neighborhood tom close to her blind.
She starts with an owl call, gets no response,
moves to soft hen purrs and clucks but he evades
her, counts his hen harem when he hears each
call to make sure no bird has gone astray.
On rainy days his covey takes to the fields;
they can't hear their enemies in woods
when rain beats leaves. He takes time from patrolling
his ridge to fight off young males
who hope to horn in on his bevy. She
notices this even in her daily defeats,
decides on the seventh day to become a he-
turkey, competitor on the strut. She hikes out
to her oak tree blind, settles in for the wait,
clutches her gobbler shaker and gobbles hard.
The old boss tom comes on the trot to defend
his territory; he doesn't see her gun.

Potato Leek Soup

Heat two tablespoons of cold pressed olive oil
in your large red enameled stockpot
over medium heat. Cut four large leeks
including the green tops, about two pounds
weight, into quarter inch thick slices and
sauté for five minutes or until they're tender.

Wild leeks taste best in this pale green soup
if they are in season and you can find them.
If it's not legal to harvest wild leeks
in the state where you live, please
use a domestic variety, of course.

Peel and cube four large, or about four cups
of russet potatoes. Add these with five
cups of water, one teaspoon of sea salt
and one half teaspoon of fresh ground pepper
to the kettle.

Cover this and bring it to a boil. Reduce
the heat to medium-low and simmer
the mixture for fifteen to twenty minutes,
or until the potatoes are tender.

Cool the soup for ten minutes. Pour the mix
from the stockpot to the blender or food
processor. Cover and puree.
Return the mix to the red pot.

Cut eight ounces of cream cheese into cubes
and whisk these into the mix a few cubes
at a time. Cook this on medium heat,
stirring constantly until the cheese melts.
Add one half cup of whole milk and heat through,
stirring occasionally.

          Sprinkle the soup
with fresh cut chives just before serving
then savor each spoonful of this meal,
in good company.

Lures

The beekeeper's wife fishes for bass. She's
seen them come up beneath ducklings, swallow
them whole, little webbed feet still paddling,
waving from the mouth of their destiny.
She believes there's nothing like the splashy
strike of an eight pound largemouth bass
as it takes a topwater lure; the cast,
a vicious strike, and a shallow-water
battle of gill-rattling jumps excites her
even more than spring honey. She uses
single-props, walking baits and poppers
in lakes and rivers fifty degrees or
warmer. She knows when water is cooler
bass are lethargic, won't rise to the surface
to feed where she can see them strike the lure,
where they are momentarily airborne,
made metallic by the sun. The skirmish
arouses her. She loves hand-painted baits,
jewel-like, shiny as any shad or
minnow water-borne for larger fish
to eat. She thinks, with their treble hooks
designed to get a barbed tip in the mouth
or gill of any fish that strikes, double-props
look more vicious than anything she wants
to do with a finned creature. Instead
she makes her Spook or Creek Walker
sashay through water in a zigzag called
"walking the dog" that fools bass
as they surface school. She gives them time
to read the menu; tempts great lunkers
by slowing her lure. She points her rod
at the fish, takes up slack line until she feels
the tug on the other end; steadies her arm
and wrist, turns her body swiftly,
sweeps the rod and sets her hook.

Ballet

I recall my blonde brother dancing
rock to rock in this river
flicking water-beaded nylon thread
over a surface laced with dragon flies
in a ballet we learned from our father,
my brother's heart in the water-dance,
mine in netting my catch.

I wade to the stony pool below
the shadow shelter of the trout.
A deer-fly dashes against my neck
and I have time to remember
my brother's need to dance,
my loss; his suicide:
his response, perhaps to mockery,
and the two-step performed
with other men's wives.

I twist, fling up my arm
and the feathered hook flies
through the air, lands upstream,
floats down to that deep blue basin
twice 'til trout takes bait
and we are tied together.

I give the fish all the shining line
it needs, stumble down river after it
head under water, head up,
rod held aloft through the white rushing
deep to a shallow hold for my feet.

I take a stand here, in Montana,
to reel in that lost beauty,
that flash of iridescence.

Lures II

The beekeeper fishes the Au Sable's
East Branch for trout. Browns and brookies
hide in dark pools and rise to spinners
and flies on light line cast carefully
as he wades the riverbed. He avoids
Opening Day when too many anglers,
like too many deer hunters, hit the wooded streams
and shores of rivers regardless of hatch,
cloud cover, frightening fish into retreat.
He favors fly fishing, respects his finned foe,
dresses for the match in tweed jacket, string tie,
and stetson pinned with lures. The beekeeper
ties flies for every hatch from Adams
to Woolly Bugger, slow-stalks the streambed
silent as leaf-float. He casts precise rod
strokes from 10 to 2 on an imaginary
clock face in the sky, lands his fly softly
on the water's surface and repeats, repeats,
repeats 'til flashing trout takes bait. He's learned
to night-fish the hex hatch, hears that *pop* like
a snook munching on prey. That *pop* addicts
anglers for life, causes dreams of flies the size
of bats, makes him rope himself to a tree,
cast to that silty hole where the Old One
drifts, awaits *hexagenia limbata*'s birth
to leap star-ward, make wake repeatedly,
until he's too full to move further
than the beekeeper's hand-tied Robert's Drake
where it lands like the last giant caddis.
This fisherman tolerates shoulder-to-shoulder
anglers just to hear that *pop* and cast
to that trout's hideout. With the fish
on his line he wants not to set the hook
too hard to return his catch to water,
lets it slip quiet from his hand to live
to lurk in shadows of water-logs, fin
gravelly hollows under the shoreline.
He desires a rematch, needs no proof
of having won this contest unless
his wife requests rainbow for supper.

Bee Husbandry

Tending bees at their hive
becomes a type of ceremony,
smoker filled with whatever is damp,
burnable and handy, smoking
incense-like to calm the buzzing.
Was this the ancient intention
of incense; to calm the masses?
Each step in its time
to open the hive; first
the top, the inner lid, brush
the hundreds of bees off the frames
of future honey, sprinkle medicated
powdered sugar over the frame tops
to protect the bees from mites,
enemies so small bees don't think
to sting them.

Dressing to tend the bees
is like dressing for a lead role
in a wedding. It's that time of year,
and even the seasoned apiarist
wears white, puts on a veil
because bees seem to think
all things moving, large, dark,
and different smelling are to be stung,
are predators. Even something seeming
to us as small as a death's head moth,
disguised in the queen bee's odor
to enter the hive at night
will be stung to death
when its perfume wears off.

This spring the beekeeper found a mouse nest
in the bottom corner of a hive box,
cleaned it out, replaced the ruined frames
with fresh wax and wire, put box on box,
inner lid then outer lid on top, stood back
to admire his handiwork and saw
the mouse return to its nesting place, then
bee-covered, run out of the hive.

Niger

Do we tell the hummingbirds to fly south
when we take in their red feeding stations
littered with drowned ants both red and black,
or do they leave without letting us know,
dress their wings and fly from this six acres
at the hint of winter in shorter days?
Do we invite the finches to stay through
the coldest days as we fill their feeder
with tiny black Niger thistle seed that,
if dropped uneaten in the herb garden
soil, sprouts small orange and yellow flowers
that dry tan and hard with prickly stems
in the fall so we gather them for dried
bouquets for the sunroom, wonder aloud
whether we should encourage this foreign-
sounding weed in our yard, and remember our
friends who once cultivated ten foot tall
African thistles behind their garage
on a small island of few residents.
These grand purple blooms were bountiful
to look at and were about to go to seed
when we stood a ladder to take photos
and asked if they would be harvested soon?
Were the neighbors concerned? Would there be
giant thistles all over the island
in Spring? What finches would peck this huge seed?
No local goldfinch is so large and
humming birds would take no interest, still head
south this time of year. No thistle seed will
keep them, nor will their brightly colored
feeding stations, however freshly filled.

Ropewalk

In New Harmony, two mazes,
one a thatch-roofed, open, outdoor factory
of spiral narrow lanes where Friends walked
the ropewalk, wove hands-full of hemp
into rope or twined it into stiff string singing
hymns at their work.

The second a living thing of boxwood hedge,
a little square house for shelter at its center,
that you may find as you wander these furled streets.
People who do not consider the Minotaur,
his sister's betrayal, sometimes get married there.
The boundary bushes once were taller than a man
but that way trapped too many. Now the hedge
is short enough for a tall woman in retreat
to look over and find her way out or further in
even without Ariadne's ball of thread to guide her
in the rain in this town of rain trees.

Small gilt blossoms glisten
in sunset as if the sky had opened and poured
a shower on these trees. From branches
mourning doves call the long evening shadows
up from the ground and cat birds mock the cats'
prowl. The cats do not seem to listen
or worry about the odd child, Asterius:
head of a bull, body of a man, son of Pasiphaë,
who shines for all, and the dazzling white bull
that rose from the sea for her father's sacrifice
to Poseidon. He was so handsome
Minos put him with his herd and slew another, excellent,
and earthly. Poseidon's revenge was the love he caused
Pasiphaë for the bull. Minos built the Labyrinth, a maze,
to hide his daughter and grandchild...perhaps it is this myth
that makes us uneasy about windings and tangles,
makes us watch for Asterius beneath the golden rain trees.
The cats know the way through all the snarls in New Harmony.

Allergy

Roses, like romantics, are obsolete
as the potted miniature pink one
in my office window, brought inside
from the porch in autumn, attacked
all over by whitefly and aphids
because there are no ladybugs
in the house. The rose's delicate leaves
with its blossoms dried, wrinkled,
dropped all over the filing cabinet, the floor.
Left with nothing blooming, in late
February, overtaken by the need
to invoke Spring, Persephone, some form of celebration,
I desperately pot tulip bulbs to fool and force
the yellow-tipped quadruple red blossoms
in the relative warmth of my living-room window.
I pot paper whites for my office, yellow daffodils
with green leaf buds already showing next
to the kitchen sink. I know
this will make me sneeze, but Spring
and all her company may never come again
unless I perform this ritual.

Marinade of Jack Rabbit

She mixes together a can of beer,
two sliced onions, some garlic cloves chopped,
a sparkle of paprika, a pinch each
of cloves and nutmeg, two large bay leaves
and a touch of tarragon, that shrub
that threatened to overcome her herb garden
last year until she cut its stems, stripped
its leaves, dried them and bagged them in small
portions, carefully labeled, for sale
in the church bazaar. When her children found
small bags of tarragon among their
Christmas presents they teased her about what
she was smoking.

She marinates two sectioned jackrabbits
in this sauce for twenty-four hours
in a sealed plastic bag, then pours
the liquid off, into her favorite
blue-and-white graniteware sauce pan to boil
and reduce to a sauce. She pours one cup of flour,
some garlic salt, onion powder, a pinch
of pepper, and three quarters of a cup
of cracker crumbs into the bag with
the rabbit pieces, seals it and shakes it
to coat the meat. As she fries them in canola oil
she thinks of how the rabbits raided
her garden nightly, eating all
the sweet sprouts, young beans and peas.
She removes the sizzling pieces with tongs
from her iron skillet to her old, yellow
majolica platter, pours the warm
sauce over the golden portions of meat
then serves this to her family with fresh
steamed asparagus and wild rice.

$$E = mc^2$$

Reading too much in a week-end
(drowning=asphyxiation by H^2O,
water, a mix, elemental chemistry
[How can we cool the cooling towers?
Where store the waste? How long?])
I surface wondering which book also
has a one-shoed man in it
or is that multi-display
large screen television?
Don't call on a cellular phone.
This is a private conversation.
Does biology=telephone?
Is it like any other team
we could field in our favor?

As a child I could only wish
atoms had not split, been smashed,
when jets cracked our windows,
learned to fly faster than sound,
dropped practice bombs called "shapes"
as if they were an innocent cure
like *blanc mange*, calf's-foot jelly,
or some other molded gelatin to sooth
the wire nerves of the universal mechanism
on its way to a super-collision
during math anxiety
when improper fractions were just
more ill-mannered numerals
while my systolic/diastolic surge,
like the tide, ripened.

DNA's high-tech hieroglyphics
in all these tenuous lives' events
add up to déjà-vu or not quite.
Details differing in space or time
How long can we continue
to listen for order in chaos?

$$E = mc^2$$

Physical scientists trying to decode
what poet-philosophers attempt to encrypt.
Matter cannot travel through space/time
to be in the same place at the same moment
but what matters? Where is it?
If $E=mc^2$ is the opposite true?
Can this relationship be reversed?
Yes, mathematically, and no, philosophically?

Are you in the equation? Caught
in the ethernet? A tourist
in cyberspace? Are you a cyborg?
Who is that on the inside of the VDT
backlit like a stageset?
A reflection of ourselves
or created in our image?
Like a file from the computer
escape through that super-cooled liquid,
the glass of the monitor's screen.
Undelete yourself.
Make this mechanism scroll forward again
with its boolean logic,
0=off, 1=on.
What does 2 do to the machine?
Does 3 equal chaos?
The elegance of the discs, hard, floppy,
like hats, French *chapeaux*.
The explicit sizes, 5¼", 3½",
wondrous math symbols containing "and,"
yes, navel gazing.

$$E = mc^2$$

Or am I out of the formula?
What keys to use, what keystrokes?
Writing, unable to speak,
unable to think fast in company.
Drained, not stimulated,
by the presence of others at 12:11 a.m.
or is it p.m.? Can you tell time
at noon or midnight? Can you tell right
from wrong on the spur of the moment
in this continuum?
Could the little death become
the great death? Petit mal become grand mal?
Lesions grow the way adhesions grow,
like cancer?
We don't have far to go
to be part of the solution.
We are almost all liquid.

Her Month

Born on a Friday in March, there are days
in her month when she feels like a young
planet Mars: active volcanoes spewing
sulfur compounds into the air. Overloads
of estrogen feel like sulfur combining
with the hydrogen and oxygen
in her environs to create sulfuric
acid and rain on everyone near her.
She's thankful that her family is not
made of limestone. Even though they are
highly carbonate, they are not destroyed
like the rocks of early Mars. She thinks of
the puzzle of the red planet named for
the god of war, and her own blue planet,
not so named and yet so warlike. Perhaps
she needs her planet to be cold and dry,
its moon-stirred oceans forever frozen.
She thinks of this as a kind of peace and prays,
Pax vobiscum. She wishes the absence
of hostility, the presence of serenity,
tranquility for all others since she
cannot achieve this for her interior self.
She hopes this calm, this conjured atmosphere,
will cool her the way the red planet is,
in spite of its color and namesake,
frozen in peace.

The Maple Wood

was deep green until
nights of chill breeze
set the trees a feverish flush,
I thought they could recover
but the weather grew colder
and their shade turned
to a blush which bled
drop by drop to the ground
until a steady rain left
a large red stain beneath
skeletons whose limbs
I could hear clattering,
summoning all souls,
proclaiming all saints,
until children came
to demand their tithe.

Pheasant

She lets Goldie out in the fields to exercise
after a long spring and summer spent
confined to the yard while birds nest, hatch
and fledge at the edge of her world.
She watches for birds as she drives to
and from school: late summer road kills, or
pheasants feeding along a drainage ditch
that look up at her as if posing for a photo
as she passes. She takes Goldie on practice
runs beating the brush for birds, fetching sticks
thrown into stubble fields and brush land.
She scouts birds flocked and gleaning harvested
farm land, ring-necks headed into briar-filled
fence rows and dense marshes, the only cover
left to them in early December. She and her Lab
hunt, light snow on the ground, trees bare-branched,
pheasants elusive, leaving only tracks
and wing-tip snow angels from flight feathers
as they land or flush, but she knows these signs
mean birds are around. The rising cackle
of a flushed cock raises the hair on the back
of her neck, makes Goldie perk up her ears
and whiff the air.

Jardin Sauvage

In October the *Journal Gazette* reports
the Department of Natural Resources request
for volunteers to gather seeds to help restore
prairie and oak savannas, the article printed
next to a column featuring recipes for salmon
smoked over applewood, cured in wintergreen,
and as a tartare with crinkleroot oil accompanied
by three pre-born fiddleheads, furled
onto a plate, one tucked in a beggar's purse
with nettle pesto, another with roasted garlic
and garlic-mustard oil, the last stuffed
with eggplant caviar, dipped in bulrush crêpe batter
and sautéed.

    As she reads these she thinks
this is a good use of the garlic-mustard that,
like kudzu in the south, has become ubiquitous
in the north. She thinks of cooking squash
with milkweed buds, steamed daylily stalks,
and quail in a reduction of wild rose hip juice.
She wonders whether burdock is a seed
the DNR needs.

    Its antecedents, cousins
to aster, daisy and sunflower, arrived
in the new world in the colonists' livestock feed,
and, like the thistle, it grows along railways
and in fallow fields where her retriever Goldie wades,
too efficiently collects these hooked hitchhikers,
burs in her underbelly fur, her waving flag tail.
The dog scratches at them until they are so entangled
they must be cut out using the kitchen scissors.
She thinks probably the state doesn't want these
insidious, dog-hairy seeds even if the parent plant's
root is still steeped by Ojibway and Potawatami
to make tea to purify their blood.

Jardin Sauvage

In spring its leaves,
 growing in a large rosette, cause her to mistake it
for rhubarb until its tight clusters of lavender florets
appear, attract bees, butterflies and soldier beetles.
In late summer the seed head forms and its burs
become tenacious barbs once used as makeshift fasteners,
naming the plant cuckoo, cockle or beggars' buttons.

She's not afraid to cook stinging nettles in a soup,
use mountain ash sprouts, redolent of almond paste,
in yogurt, wild garlic leaf oil in a sauce for fish,
wild ginger to dress tuna or cauliflower,
using just the tips, or young leaves and stems.

She knows burdock roots, raspy stalks and leaves
are edible after two boilings, with a pinch of soda
in the first one, but she's not tempted
by this *plante sauvage,* this natural velcro.

Discipline

She teaches Goldie to point, a useful
talent in a dog who retrieves wetland birds
instinctively. She wants to expand
her dog's repertoire, and her pet
capitulates, likes this new diversion
of whiffing the breeze for mourning dove,
pheasant, or quail, on the wing or scuttling
through the undergrowth. Cloud-cast early autumn
mornings are made for dog and orange-clad mistress
to shoulder through head-high corn rows to where
the harvester has done its work, where the ground
is rough with broken stalks, and doves or grouse
fly in to glean the grain and insects
fallen from dried down ears. Learning to sweep
the field for game, Goldie wants to rush in
and retrieve a bird as she would a duck
shot by her companion, but soon she learns
to stand with nose pointed and tail up-stretched
then, on command, flush the birds she's found.

She's used to gun-fire and fetching downed birds,
but unaccustomed to the tone of voices
when she's shown off to the neighbors, Amish
farmers who put electronic collars on their
blue tick hounds or weimaraners then watch
a small monitor to track them running
across the fields, chasing chicken-eating
coyotes or foxes.

Eyes focused on the ground, Goldie points
as the sportsmen move in, wings thunder,
birds erupt from the grass, shot shells explode,
and a dove falls, leaves a cloud of feathers
in the sky. She races to retrieve the bird,
cradles it gently between her teeth,
carries it back, smartly turns and sits
at her mistress's feet. She holds the still warm,
feathered creature until commanded
to release her prize.

Thinking about high school

and reunions in Michigan
reminds me of that unlit stretch of 131
north of Constantine
where semis pass each other going ahead of me
and when they've cleared the oncoming lane
the headlights of the traffic blind me
so a large rural mailbox looming
out of the nightyard on my right
looks like a deer about to leap
in front of my car while I make plans
for an accident where something natural
and something unnatural are about to collide
and I think I have it fixed in my mind
which is which but adrenaline flows
and I'm past and recognizing the box
when I speak sharply to the loud boy
in the back seat.

Cochineal II

She wears a deep red turtleneck sweater
through the holidays, develops a rash
on her shoulders, arms and chest, but doesn't
know she's reacting to the cochineal
saturated yarn of her new sweater.

She remembers the symptoms from a trip
to the southwestern desert where she touched
the silvery scale-like insect patch
on a prickly-pear cactus. Learned about
the delicate *plateada,* its careful
cultivation by the Indians.

She recalls the burgundy chenille bedspread
she napped on as a child at her grandmother's
house. How, in summer, she would perspire
and wake up with hives from the dye called
carmine, made from the cochineal. She cried
and scratched, was spanked for crying and
scratching.

Now, her tears fall as she puts her new
Christmas sweater in the washing machine,
tries to undo some of the vigilance
and hard work of her cousins.

Head On

Her friend Carol was worried about
her mother beginning to forget things:
her keys, her purse, her location:
then she heard the radio news
mention the possible pact
between several men, very ill,
who climbed into a small plane one day
to crash deliberately, to die. Weeks later
what were her mom and those three
bridge club ladies in their eighties thinking
when they left Milford on a sunny,
20° January morning to go to lunch?
All in Millie's '86 Caddy, no airplane,
they headed north on State Road 15, discussing
their heart attacks and hip replacements
they navigated Goshen's snowy streets
safely, drove on through Elkhart
not stopping to shop at Walmart or
the mall, chatting all the way
about grown children, grandchildren,
their friend Marge in Nappanee,
Betty from Bremen who moved
to Syracuse, their departed
husbands, *Bruce was so stupid, James was
a gem, a real provider.* These women
had traded secrets for begetting, or not,
traded *rumtopf* and sourdough starter.
She wonders whether they had an accident
or an agreement when their north-going car
met an east-going, left-turning, semi-
tractor-with-trailer at a high rate
of speed at the accident prone
intersection of State Road 15
and SR 20 in Mishawaka
or Elkhart. Carol says it's hard to tell
just which South Bend suburb it is
right there, where their souls debarked.

Dominion

We swallow spiders in our sleep
a recent survey says; not just one
per year for those of us who slumber
on our backs, mouths open to breathe,
to snore. Why doesn't the spider suspended
on its silky filament simply haul
itself away from danger? Does the dark,
damp, gaping, human maw tempt,
seem too much like a possible home site,
a place where insects could be trapped
for dinner? When I am awake I don't find
numerous bugs haunting the neighborhood
of my mouth even, or especially, when it's open.
What winged members of this food chain
fly by our facial environs in night
while we dream of Venus Fly-traps, or spiders,
that signify pure happiness when
we see them in our night visions,
as if we must imagine arachnids
to balance the high? Don't look up
at the stippled stucco ceiling; spiders
and their dinner companions hide
behind every little plaster stalactite. Trying
to ignore the threat of inhaled ephemera
I tuck myself in bed, hunt the waffle-weave
thermal blanket from where it retreats
down between sheet and comforter. The comforter,
large, soft-stuffed object that, by multiplying
my own warmth, attempts to compensate
for the lack of other heat, other comfort,
in my four-poster, queen-sized,
but who can think herself a queen
with no subjects, no king, no consort?
I bury my cold nose under the top edge
of my blankets. This hides my bug-trap
of a mouth but puts me in close proximity
to the sources of dust-mites; my pillow, my mattress.

Dominion

These tiny millions dine on fallen flakes of flesh,
not allergic to humans the way we can be
allergic to cats even when they play
with spiders – toss them as they would a mouse,
pounce on the disoriented arachnids,
like they toss and hop after those large moths
my grandmother called millers because
they are dusty like the faces and clothes
of mill-hands. Mites would love to sleep
with those guys. But these specks
will be snorted, snuffed up into my sinuses,
make me sneeze, perhaps expel
an errant spider from my throat. What errand
is the eight-legged on, what hunt,
when it lowers itself on its lifeline
to my face? Wouldn't it benefit
from acquaintance with dust-mites,
the size and numbers of which must be
to the spider as the ocean of plankton
is to the whale? I pray silently, make a vow,
a plan, cast a spell against the multitudes
of minutiae, my only domain.

Sweat

The beekeeper sweats
while he works the hive,
boxes heavy with wax-filled frames
and maybe some honey
as he transfers their weight
to his legs and lifts them,
one for each colony,
into place over a metal grid:
a queen excluder
between lower brood chambers
and upper honey harvest boxes.
It is almost always
a hot time of year to do this,
add the double layers of clothing
for protection, the heavy shoes
and hat and gloves, because bees
go for any crevice in the intruder's
clothes and then the crease in the neck,
behind the ear, or next to the veined nose
as if they can smell the sweat
emerge from fleshy pores
from all the sources of perspiration:
muscle strain, stress, fear,
and the work of loving the hive,
doing what the colony needs,
or as if human musk attracts bees.

PT
YOU
K YOU
2018 10-17AM
00#2240
LOCAL AUTHOR
MDSE ST
TAX1
ITEMS
***TOTAL
CASH
CHANGE

01
CLERK01
$12.32
$12.32
$0.74
10
$13.06
$15.00
$1.94

The Hunt

as somber about last Saturday
eekeeper and I walked down the hill
jon-boat lay on its side
ain drained out except
d charcoal-colored mouse
up at us when we tipped
the boat upright to install oars
and ourselves. He had been rolled
on his back with the turn of the boat
so we saw his cream underside clean
as a white china plate before he twisted
and righted himself.   His dark tail was half-
again as long as his body where every hair
was sleeked in place as he stopped still.
Long-legged spiders scattered and ran
for grass as the beekeeper slid a paddle under
the fear-frozen rodent and lifted him into the yard.
Placed near the base of a lake willow,
the long tail and its owner disappeared
in the dapple of the woods beside the channel.
I hoped for its life, thought of our black-and-white cat;
Katie rarely brings us a mouse among the voles,
house finches, and young rabbits she drops
on the mat by the back door for our admiring
congratulations. She yeows outside
until she has our attention, then tosses
her catch and jumps at it, re-enacts the hunt.
It seems she can't instruct us often enough
to make great stalkers of us, and this Saturday
when we returned from our rowing
the hind-quarters and lengthy tail
were what remained of the gift
of a dark gray mouse on the back porch.

Shanda Hansma Blue

Hunting Seasons

As we stop the car abruptly to steal
a look at the flock of turkeys about
to step in our way, they are silk, glimmer
ebony-blue, stand a few yards from this
gravel road, across the ditch among scrub trees
and those low bushes of wild blueberries.
Their fabric shines like iridescent black
feathers, but these birds don't move, don't turn
to flee from our halted vehicle where we watch
through the windows, driver and passenger,
husband and wife. He lowers the window
nearest the birds *He puts my window down,*
they make no sound so he gobbles at them

while I remember visiting Sylvia
when she won a turkey-hunting license
in the state lottery and insisted
on giving me a shooting lesson,
not with her birthday gift, matte-black rifle
just for turkey hunting *Shiny objects*
frighten them, but with a duck-hunting
video game on the t.v. I surprise myself
and do OK. She says she knew I would.

But today, as he and I search
for a mushroom hunting spot, we hear that
gobble-gobble-gobble nearby, look
to the sound we think another bird,
but see, camouflaged, a small green-and-brown tent,
a hunting blind behind these sightless turkeys.

Deer Song

A yearling doe patrols
our yard in snow cover. Dawn
to dusk as far as we can tell. She
browses our bulb garden for tulip shoots,
scrapes the snow and myrtle aside
next to the split rail fence; there must be
some green nutritious thing sprouting beneath.
I go out to sing *Kitty kitty kitty*,
in the way French shop clerks chirp
Bonjour, Madame; Bonjour Monsieur,
and there she stands looking at me
from behind the junipers, below
the bird feeder. She doesn't even flinch,
so I imagine she has grown up
in our woods, has heard my cat calling
every day of her life, has perhaps seen me
when I didn't see her as I retrieved
house pets.
            When snow is very deep
we put hay out to distract the deer
from eating the young red buds
and arbor vitae, and find the bales
also harbor rabbits for the winter;
we sing back to the finches and cardinals
as we fill the feeders. Each evening
we read or doze under the lamplight
while the yellow-and-white kitten runs
quickly to a corner in the kitchen
and listens to an electrical outlet
in the wall outside of which hangs
the porch swing, near the picnic table.
Perhaps the doe shelters on that patio,
or a homeless cat or possum that Fuzz
hears wheezing in the cold night
next to the house. I don't know
what to sing, what key to use,
to call the deer close enough
to touch more than sight.

Switch

I hear that *pop* come from under the dash;
not the same noise my friend Lynn heard when the deer,
the second deer, not the first deer, hit her passenger side
front car door and left his rack dangling from the hole he made.
She was embarrassed to have to report this second run-in
on U.S.33 in six months, but glad to have the antlers to prove it.
This *pop* isn't that dangerous sound;
then the dash lights go out, all but two,
and I think that's the only problem.
An inconvenience in this night-driving thunderstorm
until the state trooper pulls me over
half an hour later between Wabash and Elwood.
Something about Wabash makes me feel violated anyway
though it should be Elwood, home of the KKK,
that makes me feel that way. I always feel lucky
to get through that town. I see flashing lights
in my rear-view and check my speed (one of the two lights).
I still have plenty of gas. But I feel I am attracting
undue attention for I-don't-know-what reason
as the officer walks up to my window
during a lull in the storm
and asks to see my driver's license.
I dig it out of my wallet before I think to ask
Is something wrong?
I hope this doesn't make me late
to pick up my son. *You have no taillights.*
Oh. *I heard the fuse go just south of Pierceton*
but I thought it was only the dash lights.
I don't tell him about Lynn's two deer adventures.
He looks like he's trying to appear authoritative
and to be politically correct at the same time. I wonder

Switch

whether he studies this expression in the mirror at home
in the morning before he takes off for work,
maybe after he shaves, before breakfast. I hope
he doesn't practice this face on his kids. He seems young
so I think he has small children who would be scared
by this look from their dad. *How far you going tonight?*
I'm picking my son up in Indianapolis
and going on to Bloomington. He gives me a warning
ticket and tells me to watch for cars coming up behind me,
tap my foot on the brake to show them I'm there,
and show the ticket to any troopers who pull me over
so they don't give me another *for your taillights anyway.*
I laugh and thank him and say I'll change the fuse
when I get to my ex's. I don't explain that this is
my second ex-husband who sometimes seems
glassy-eyed as Lynn's dazed second deer.
I turn on the dome light and pull away. My son
and I change the fuse a couple of times
in the pouring-down rain before we get the message:
maybe there's a dead short in the system. My ex
asks me what I'm going to do. I'm not sleeping
at his house tonight. *I'll get my car fixed*
when I get back to Kalamazoo.
You can't do that!
I'll turn the dome light on. None of us thinks
of the emergency flashers. I don't remind him
about Lynn's two deer hits with her brand new
car the year of our first separation. She said the deer
bounded away into the twilight like
the ghost of a deer – any whitetail –
because he was no longer crowned. Gray and I leave.
People on 465 flash their lights, honk and gesture,
sometimes appear to lose control of their own cars
in their efforts to tell us our taillights are out.

Bargain

Browsing the pow-wow, comparing the arts
of dream-weavers, I'm on my second round
through the booths when I see the catcher hung
with hands-full of light brown downy feathers
separating royal blue beads, a tiny turquoise
woven into the center. Meant to be mine,
it is suspended at one end of a long booth
but I'm a thorough shopper today;
Rooster feathers the trader from Jemez Pueblo says
when I ask whether the shiny, sleek, black quills
of the dream-catcher at the other end of his booth
are crow. I love the other one
but might buy this jet-necklace-colored thing
just to own crow-hued feathers
or to give a friend. Even I know
rooster feathers are not usually for women.
My grandfather always said of loud girls,
A whistling woman is like a crowing hen.
The shape and color of these quills say *macho, death,*
not *light* or *life.* I move back to the catcher
with a small chartreuse stone caught in its weft.
Web trimmed with brown speckled tufts of down
from those prairie chickens whose roosters
have brilliant yellow-gold feathers
on cheeks that they puff up to attract
females. Tied up with bouquets of feathers
adorned with lucent blue glass beads, it vows
to tangle the wings of all my bad dreams.
I'll take this one, please, I say when he makes
his way back to me. I ask the price and the trader
points to each of the catchers he has seen
me touch, tells me the cost. I do not haggle,
but when he asks my name, writes the receipt,
he gives me a break anyway, and I whistle on.

Cacophony

The '86 Ford Escort wagon stalled at the light
at the corner of *La Revolución* and *El Presidente*
in Tijuana attracts little attention even loaded
as it is with six beautiful young Mexican men,
each dressed in a ruffled white shirt, an elaborate
gold, red, orange, or blue bow at the throat.
As the light turns green the Mariachi band,
unable to make the car go, disembarks
to the delight of the large-beaked Macaw
perched on the saddle of the zebra-striped
donkey harnessed to the corner photo stand's cart
under a chartreuse and fuchsia sign
that says TIJUANA 1999 MEXICO in the shade
of two royal palms near where we stand
chatting in the sun as crowds of out-of-school
local kids and tourists swarm past us;
I want you to climb up on the donkey cart,
sit under the sign, have your photo taken with me
because we see each other so seldom
this might be our last act in the century
and should be commemorated by something
more charming than our full bellies
from too many good restaurants in one long weekend
in San Diego, but even your visits to apparently
poor, crowded, Mexican towns disconcert you.
You want no evidence left for posterity
so we smile into each other's eyes
and raise our voices in chorus
as we avoid eye contact with the proprietor
of the Macaw-and-donkey cart while the bird flaps
his clipped wings and screams *Vámonos!* at the boys
in tight black pants who scramble from the Escort,
push it through the intersection
where everything with wheels and horns
in the vicinity plays a symphony
in cacophony to accompany, deride,
encourage, or chide the Mariachis.

Still

Before we went to sleep
you said you didn't want to go home,
back to Michigan, didn't believe me
when I said *I feel movement here*
all the time. Black-capped chickadees
and sparrows in their plain brown wrappers,
celebrations of everything dappled,
sweep the crumbs from the tile floor
near the glass hacienda doors
and tidy the palm fronds woven
in the carpet of El Cafe Picante
at a beach formed by a man-made inlet
of the Pacific. Orange Birds-of-Paradise
stick out purple tongues to catch hummingbirds
who flirt with my red shirt. At my table in the sun
of the veranda I write, waiting for you
to join me beneath these shaggy palms.
The waitress is too attentive, doesn't understand
this penciling person who eats so slowly;
she wants to know the story behind such poor
attention to the melons, strawberries, bananas
and kiwi slices of the heaped fruit plate. *Waiting*
for a friend; will be here for a while, I say,
so she assures me I need not feel rushed
as I write about yesterday afternoon in Tijuana
but not last night's earthquake. I was awake
when the tremors started at almost 3 a.m.;
this morning the T.V. news said seven-point-two
on Cal Tech's Richter scale, its center
at a small desert town named after a cactus
called Joshua Tree. When the bed's shaking
awakened you I grabbed your hand to keep you
from getting up, stumbling around
the swaying fifth floor hotel room. I wanted you
to remember you were not alone. As the room rocked
and rolled you said you had changed your mind
because *Home, though cold, usually holds still.*

Bouquet

The wind is still until one-fifteen
when the afternoon breeze begins to toss
the top branches of the eucalyptus trees,
then the lower cedars and spruces
start to move. Long, aromatic leaves
rustle and fall like large raindrops hitting
the lawn. The rising wind prompts the limbs
and dry leaves to sounds like the lake
at Syracuse quietly bumping boats
against the docks while little waves lap
the stanchions, the uprights, of the piers there.
Does the wind excite the coyotes?
They begin to call in the foothills further east
and all the dogs in the neighborhood yap
nervously to each other. The horse down the hill
perks her ears and canters around her paddock.
Unlike their one a.m. barking, the peacocks
across the dusty gravel lane take no notice.
By two-thirty this afternoon honey bees
busily cruise the herbs and flowers
in the border gardens as Sam,
the resident marmalade tabby, dozes
on the shaded grass beneath my lawn chair
keeping company on *El Cajon*.

Lydia Crocheting in the Garden

The beekeeper's wife visits the art institute
where she looks at a painting of Miss Cassatt
whose blue dress, edged with multi-colored embroidery,
in its brightness and impressionistic detail
is the most *present* object in the painting. Her red
sash is a nice contrast with her frock and the azure
lacy shawl she works at with her brass hued crochet
hook. The fichu is for Corabella, Elsie's cherished
doll. Her niece asked her to make something
of two handfuls of nearly crushed pink rose petals,
but Lydia declined, explained their fragile nature
and volunteered this marine blue cotton yarn
for the doll's covering. In this painting Miss Cassatt
is even more pallid than that porcelain plaything:
her face a near transparency, as if she disappears
as Mary paints her. Her white lace bonnet is imbued
with those pinkish highlights the month of May uses
to soften the evanescing of white on many
a healthy complexion. Perhaps it is just the effect
of the shade cast upon her face beneath the hat,
but even her tea-with-milk colored gloves,
the backs of which she has carefully embroidered
with three bright red lines, are not so pale. Mary records
this detail as she captures the contemplative soul
buried within these clothes, fading in this face.
Were those gloves worn by living hands, or is that
an illusion? Is her ashen face all that is left
of Lydia?

The Grand Tour

In her dream of the Cassatt exhibit
Lydia Cassatt escapes her illness and obligation
to sit for her sister as iron rails soften into song.
How to stay awake, go on? There is always thirst:
that train taking her in search of dreamed water.
Her knitting needles counterpoint the click, clack
of the rail carriage wheels through the dry country
outside Madrid where there is only economy;
grandmothers sweep the streets so clean
there is little for a pigeon to glean, few birds
for cats to stalk. Her fingers work the yarn
in syncopated rhythm to the sway of the train
all the way to central Italy where, in the courtyards
of Arrezzo, large clay pots with spiral floors,
and small holes for air and light along their sides,
house herds of dormice saved from felines.
These mice are fed as much as they can eat, fattened
for human fodder, eaten roasted and dipped in honey
and sesame seeds. Tracking the coast she chooses
Mediterranean blue yarn for the next section
until she arrives in Venice where there is one
herring gull that hunts and kills three or four
pigeons a day, better than the thousands
of wild tabbies in the city of canals can do.
Back on the train she tries to crochet an afghan
with perfect vanished seams the way DNA
and genes knit a seamless convoluted brain,
the way memory needles a life into what we want
to have happened; not leaving out events but hiding
some in folds and seams invisibly. Not biography,
or portraiture, but that subjective story:
the way a dove looks like part of the sculpture
as it hangs its head over the small spigot of a fountain,
then it moves to touch beak to water.

Shangri La

Why do the black-necked cranes of Bhutan
mate for life when that could be eighty years?
What do the younger Buddhist monks think
as they hang from the open temple windows
beneath the overhang of the red tile roof to watch
the cloud of cranes circle them thrice on their return
in Spring? Do the healers among the monks
contemplate their late summer harvest
of flowering remedies on the rocky slopes? Or
do they entertain themselves with thoughts
of the hornbills who mud their mates
into the hollow of a tree trunk during nesting
season? Why do Buddhists think these birds
an example of gracious selflessness?
Does the hornbill's mate appreciate his flight
from tree to tree testing fruit for ripeness
with his huge beak gently? Does he hear
her knocking her beak against the narrow mud
opening in her hideaway? Does the snow-leopard
hear, she who is no longer white at this time of year?
Does the sound distract her from her hunt
of goat antelope kids? Do the golden langurs
born for the monkey-life in the deepest-green-
top-most canopy take note? Would they come down
to earth if they did? From their home
can they see eagles and vultures dropping
the largest bones on stones to break
and spill their marrow?
Would we give our corpses to the monks
to be dismembered and laid generously
on a rocky outcropping mountainside,
to feed the birds? For sky burial?

Revision

That dead beagle lying in the gravel beside the railroad crossing
as my car tops the rise over the tracks distracts me from the sign
I see each morning on the way to a job where I am no more, or less
secure than any other woman who sells her time. It says TRAINS
DON'T WHISTLE in concert with the anti-noise ordinance in Elkhart,
Indiana, where we don't want to frighten the horses pulling Amish
buggies, but I don't see it today because I look at the dog and wish
for crows, buzzards, remember domesticity. I want that carcass recycled
immediately by carrion eaters in the Buddhist way, not the way
we recycle cans and bottles, paper and plastic. Not dead stuff into more
dead stuff but the way flesh feeds flesh, the living eat the recently live
to keep life in themselves. Remember domesticity; an elderly couple
caught at the other side of the crossing, unable to see what I see,
await the passing train and revise the search for their dog.

Scan

I lie in the tunnel of the magnetic resonance imaging machine, the sting
of a generated breeze on my tongue, the scales
of rock music in my ears as well as the pounding of low "C"
notes. The machine prepares its resounding vibration. It pivots,
revolves around my prone self. *Lie perfectly still,* the attendant seems to wheeze.
Perhaps he, too, is allergic to autumnal fungi or yellowing birch

leaves. I am nervous, resistant, but don't need the whip of a birch
branch to convince me of this test. The suggestion, the scent, the sting
of potential disease or nerve damage is enough to keep me from weaseling
out of this day's exam. I hadn't reckoned with noise, the scale
monotonous, reverberating. I close my eyes against the dim lights – a pivotal
thought thinks me out of here, perhaps to Heaney's Irish sea

coast, where the rye waves in the breeze again. I can almost see
the green, smell it, but I am tired and my mind turns to the white birch's
delicate branch and foliage, an equal beauty, leaves pivoting
in the moving air. All its image behind my eyelids relieves stress even as stinging
memory of last evening's leaf smoke reminds me of the season, the scale
of color of soon to be empty trees. How the squirrels, raccoons, weasels

dig in for the coming cold the way I am in this bunker like the weasel's
burrow only better lit, ventilated. I wish I could see
a dozen white tulips and hear my daughter's violin singing its scales
practiced in our livingroom for years but the MRI sounding and the birch
of my imagination are interference, seduction. The smell, stinging,
of paper-whites and allergy in my nose creates a spasm – my body pivots,

contorts slightly. The winter of the chile ristra hung from a pivotal
pot hook on the ceiling rack in my kitchen made my eyes burn, lungs wheeze
until I discovered the problem of the dried chiles and carried the string
out to the back porch, opened doors and windows for a sea-
change. At the following year's end it was the paper-whites in a birch-
stump planter that caused the allergic bronchitis on a grand scale.

Scan

Now the MRI is louder, sound and rhythm suitable for "La Scala"
in a much larger venue than this body-sized niche with its pivoting
image-making electro-magnets. It imprints the details of my spine on film like birch
bark in its delicacy and contrast while I concentrate not to wheeze
with asthma – no panic here – no fear of small places, screams in the higher notes of "C"
as I think of a way to reward my own good behavior later … perhaps a stringer

of trout to scale for breakfast, though a campfire, too, can make me wheeze.
What could be important, even pivotal, would be a trip to the sea,
west coast, my sister's house, no birches, but in her yard eucalyptus odor stings.

Patience

When Tillie leaves the kitchen, Carl, where he sits
at the table finishing his supper, confides
to his daughter-in-law, *The woman who lives here*
is stealing his railroad checks. He wants to go home
to his momma in his dementia. She misses
the flirt of his calling her *Honey Bunch*, saying
it's about time his son had some happiness
in his life. Carl was a compulsive mower,
plower of snow and spring garden, a man
of quick runs to town in his pick-up, a honker
of the car horn when not quite waiting for Tillie
to go to church. Then he saw lions in the fields,
plowed his cane under with the corn stalks, escaped
the house to walk their rural road in the dead
of night, *Someone's at the door. Someone needs help.*
Someone's here to rob us. After the tiny strokes
give way to a massive one, and heart attack,
he lies, taking his ease among the electrodes,
the tubing and machinery of the intensive care
ward. His young nurse wakes the son and his wife
where they sleep on the couches of a waiting-room,
It's time; the end is very close, and they walk down
the hall to hold his hand, say goodbye yet again.
The daughter-in-law leans, whispers in his ear,
It's okay; it's time to go home to Momma.
He sighs; his rigid form relaxes and he is gone.

Internal Bleeding

Those ovoid fuzzy green containers that are
poppy buds filled with wrinkled red petals,
the way something green bleeds inwardly,
the outward green of rhubarb that is red
and tart inside, the way everything feminine
bleeds, sometimes with the sweetness of Sangria,
a drink for fiestas, or the thirty gallon galvanized
tin livestock watering tub full of red wine, fruit juice,
and ice I mixed up for friends Memorial Day weekend,
1973, when my twenty-two month-old daughter
made an afternoon's adventure of finishing off
what was left in the bottoms of plastic glasses,
so I put her to bed in her crib, drunk. Last winter
I lost something in a beat up old two-toned cranberry pick-up
so for months every red truck and certain shades
of sunlit brown attract my sight. I read the personals
because what can be found there is the difference
between men and women; who they think they are,
who they want. My heart is a pocket with a hole
in it. All the doctors say they hear the murmur,
ask me whether I'm often out of breath. Of course,
but I don't want tests, I'm not ready for stitches
to fix what works. I have not found a heart-
or pocket-shaped herb to cure this internal flow
and shush-hush, this fissure only men fall through.

For Lilacs

For more than twenty years I could say my
lilac bush, my garden. Should have said our
yard, our house, because we were, and knew why
we were, there for many of those days, hours.
Like the trumpet vine in our back yard, green
shoots springing up through the grass, no boundaries,
no guards at the borders could stop its keen
urge to proliferate. Our corollary
drive to multiply brought forth our daughter,
dark eyed, brunette sprite, uncontainable,
born weeks before her time, a new Otter
for my great-grandmother; unrestrainable,
when she could walk she ran for the front door,
outside, purple lilacs she couldn't ignore.

For over twenty years I could say my
lilac bush, my rambling rose, my hybrids,
even that spring of the prom weekend, sky-
filling snow, covering blooms, quieting katydids.
It made the world pastel, paled green grass
and purple lilacs with a thick white veil,
subdued sounds around the neighborhood as
gowns were pressed, attention paid to details;
corsages, boutonnieres, reservations
for dinner. Parent-photographers shot
too many pictures, no revelations
in these scenes, no news, just forget-me-nots
in bloom again, teens trying to grow up,
my oldest daughter putting on make-up.

For something near twenty years our lilac
bush stood guard over the sand box, swing set.
stood between our children, grassy back-
yard, and the lake, where our babies were not yet
ready to swim without the company

For Lilacs

of watchful parents, could not go fishing
without someone to bait their hooks. Any
sunny day was good for childish wishing
to *go to the park, Mom, go swimming, Mom,*
and off we would go trailing our three cats,
black cocker spaniel, beach towels, floating flotsam
in the forms of toys, fishing gear, worms, hats
to keep the sun from burning those young faces
while children played, wove their snake-grass necklaces.

Since long before we bought this house, this half
acre surrounded on three sides by the maple-lined
village streets, the nine foot height and seven foot
width of lilac bush stood guard, anchored the yard,
was the corner post and foundation of a living
u-shaped hedge of rose ramblers, trumpet vine,
rose of sharon, yucca, and hundreds of grape
hyacinths in spring. The purple lilac stood
between the sandbox, swing set, and Front Street,
Syracuse Lake. The bush and hedge sheltered
rabbits, robins, and springtime duck nests.
Easter eggs were sometimes found there
and even on rainy days our children dragged
picnic blankets under the branches
in lieu of a tree house. Each Mother's Day
we watched for the mother duck parade
as from hidden nests the Mallards led early
new-hatched ducklings from under hedges,
and out of basement window-wells,
across Front Street to their first swim practice,
in training for independence.

Three Bees

These could be any kind of bees
or hornets, I can't differentiate.
For each of three days in a row
I find one bee on the lace curtains
of my balcony window: one of those
large, glass, sliding doors. Each day
I wonder how the stinging winged bits
of saffron got in my apartment. I think
I let them in when I go out to water
the potted plants that are my garden.
I could think of them as individual
buzzing furies but to what effect?
What's one mythological fury compared
to the hordes of worries of being a parent,
a grandparent? What's one bee clinging
to the window side of the lace where
I can just open the screen door and
let it fly? How does that compare
to parenting a bi-polar daughter?
And the next day a new bee
that I carefully encourage out the door
compares in what way to my daughter's
three year old son raising himself?
The following afternoon's warning drone
at the window-door does not add to,
or subtract from, receiving no phone calls
from a grown child so sick she usually
phones daily to ask whether she can shower
now, what dish might she take to a picnic,
what should she wear to work,
will I talk her through her son's
supper, bath, bedtime?

Light at Dusk

Not concerned with reflection or refraction
but the intensity of color just at dusk
or after the refreshment of an afternoon rain
before the sun returns full strength
when grass and trees are at their greenest
in spring, before they have gathered that dust
that doesn't wash off in summer,
no dried brown edges, but greenest green
to every perimeter, maple leaf, oak,
pointed tulip spikes, grass blade after blade.
In this light daffodils and grape hyacinth
are most yellow and purple before they fade
and are mowed, tulips are whitest, reds
are deepest while children's voices carry
clearest and farthest in the remnant humidity.
In this reflection I hear my grandson's voice
as he says his name, *Guthrie*, or mine, *Grandma*,
and makes them the same sound the way he makes
Morgan, his aunt, my daughter, and *water* sound
alike; one refreshes with humor, the other
with elemental chemistry, both necessary
to his world as he runs the length
of deepest green garden, arms waving
as if to take flight, to lighten the dusk.

One Hour After Sunset

She looks for the Pleiades star cluster
four lunar diameters above the moon.
Its glare forces her to use binoculars
to see the faint group. Hyades,
a more diffuse cluster and harder
to recognize, is ten degrees below
and slightly left of the man-in-the-moon.
She wants to put on its glowing gossamer
for an evening gown, sure it will impart
some beauty to her pale visage. Her escort
is Perseus, the Hero, in whose
constellation the Alpha star is Mirfak.
Three degrees above that this night
the Comet Machholz perches. The brilliant
moon again obscures the view until
she uses her binoculars to see
the comet with its downward pointing tail
as it passes close to Earth, journeys on
toward our sun. She dreams of the Red
Planet, then low in the southeast, an hour
before sunrise, she sees the rising
luminosity of Mars that she views
as a predictor of things to come
in her astrological year.

CPSIA information can be obtained
at www.ICGtesting.com
Printed in the USA
LVOW03s1708300418
575398LV00002B/348/P

9 781770 670693